Copyright © 2021 by Prism Vibes

All rights reserved. No part of this publication may be reproduced, distributed, or transmitted in any form or by any means, including photocopying, recording, or other electronic or mechanical methods, without the prior written permission of the publisher, except in the case of brief quotations embodied in critical reviews and certain other noncommercial uses permitted by copyright law. For permission requests, email the author, subject line "Attention: Chakra Pride Permissions" at info@prismvibes.com.

Prism Vibes

North Carolina, US 28270

www.prismvibes.com

Ordering Information:

For details, contact info@prismvibes.com.

Print ISBN: 978-0-578-98940-2

eBook ISBN: 978-0-578-99045-3

First Edition

Hello there, little one. I wrote this book to remind you of the power you have. No matter how big or small you are, know that you are more powerful than you can imagine. Inside each of us are energy centers called chakras. They act like our inner heroes, giving us superpowers to live happy, healthy, and successful lives.

Crown Chakra

Flying high above your head
Is where this energy lies,
Helping you connect to the Universe,
Your forever allies.

If you ever feel incomplete
Or unsure of your path,
Just think of me floating above,
Protecting you from any wrath.

Now I have a mantra just for you,
Repeat three times
And this will get you through.

Mantra

I know I have a purpose in this world

Third Eye Chakra

The space between your brows
Is where this energy lies,
Helping you to see beyond
The things of this world that arise.

If you ever feel afraid of your truth or reality,
Just think of me helping you to trust,
While guiding you to the truth you don't see.

Now I have a mantra just for you,
Repeat three times
And this will get you through.

Mantra
I see the truth in all things

Throat Chakra

The nook at the bottom of your neck
Is where this energy lies,
Helping you to speak your truth and express
The real you, no matter your size.

If you ever feel silenced
Or judged for what you say,
Just think of me helping you speak
Your truth anyway.

Now I have a mantra just for you,
Repeat three times
And this will get you through.

Mantra
I speak my truth and it supports and empowers me

Heart Chakra

In the middle of your chest
Is where this energy lies,
Helping you to love and connect
To all of the things under the skies.

If you ever feel lonely
Or disconnected from you,
Just think of me helping you create
Love and compassion from the sacred anew.

Now I have a mantra just for you,
Repeat three times
And this will get you through.

Mantra
I love that I am able to connect to myself and others

Solar Plexus Chakra

Right above your bellybutton
Is where this energy lies,
Helping you to know and recognize your worth,
As something that never dies.

If you ever feel small or out of place,
Just think of me helping you feel valued,
Giving you your right to take up space.

Now I have a mantra just for you,
Repeat three times
And this will get you through.

Mantra
I can achieve my life's purpose

Sacral Chakra

Just below your belly
Is where this energy lies,
Helping you to express
Your creativity and emotions that rise.

If you ever feel shame
Or can't express who you are,
Just think of me helping to remind you
That you are the main star.

Now I have a mantra just for you,
Repeat three times
And this will get you through.

Mantra
I feel myself becoming more self-expressive

Root Chakra

At the base of your spine
Is where this energy lies,
Helping you feel safe and secure
No matter what life has in surprise.

If you ever feel ungrounded or not brave,
Just think of me helping you float
On the peaks and troughs of life's ocean wave.

Now I have a mantra just for you,
Repeat three times
And this will get you through.

Mantra

I am grounded by the knowing of the divine security

When sickness or imbalances start to preside,
Consider using the energy of your chakras
To get them to subside.

Repeating mantras is a practice you can apply,
Which unblocks the power of your chakras,
They are your inner heroes, on which you can rely.

See each of these chakras are a part of you,
They connect your mind, body, and spirit,
So you can be whole and stay true.

Chakra Pride

I hope this book has helped you unlock your very own special powers. When you feel like you need a little extra help dealing with a struggle, use the mantras and what you learned in this book. They will help to activate your superhero power. If you didn't understand all the lessons, don't worry. One day it will all make sense. When it does, you will be able to help yourself and others access inner power.

CPSIA information can be obtained
at www.ICGtesting.com
Printed in the USA
LVHW070300271221
706779LV00003B/12